© 2019 by Heritage Publishing
Nashville, Tennessee

All rights reserved. No portion of this book may be reproduced, stored in a retrieval system, or transmitted in any form or by scanning, or other except for brief quotations in critical review.

Published in Nashville, Tennessee, by Heritage Publishing

Library of Congress Cataloging-in-Publishing   2017942270

ISBN   9781732072206

TABLE OF CONTENTS

Foreword		7
Chapter One	What Is a 2Man?	9
Chapter Two	Do You Know?	11
Chapter Three	Types of 2s	18
Chapter Four	The Qualities of a 2	23
Chapter Five	The Motivations of a 2	27
Chapter Six	Critical Success Tools	31
Chapter Seven	What About Me?	35
Chapter Eight	The 2Man and His Family	39
Chapter Nine	Final Reflections	42

FOREWORD

Joseph is one of my favorite biblical characters. His life story is recorded in the Old Testament. He was creative, visionary, strategic, grounded, and wise. His strategic leadership and business acumen not only positioned the Egyptian government to prosper during an economic downturn, it also spared the life of his family, who happened to be God's chosen people.

I believe the genius of it all is that Joseph did this sitting in the "second chair." He didn't occupy the role of a senior leader but accomplished more, impacted more, and experienced more than many senior leaders will in their lifetime. His life and ministry are a profound picture of the power of the "two." He had no ambition for other roles and made no attempts to occupy them. He simply bloomed where he was planted; and as a result, God's kingdom was expanded, his family was provided for, and God got the glory.

In an era of unprecedented exposure to the accomplishments of others, many leaders have become confused about their assignments. It is as if this exposure has created an appetite of ambition that often undervalues the power of finding their lane, living in their lane, and loving their lane. This is what this amazing book is about. This work reminds the Josephs of the world that your contribution to businesses, churches, and government is invaluable. You are a gift to the world and a special gift to people like me.

I've had the blessing and privilege of having Ramone Harper as a Joseph for over a decade. My life and our organization would not be the same without him. The content contained in these pages isn't just a message he has written; it's a message he has lived. May the words on these pages bless you the way his life and service have blessed me.

Dr. Dharius Daniels
Senior Leader, Change Church

CHAPTER ONE

WHAT IS A 2MAN?

"It takes 2 to make a thing go right! It takes 2 to make it out of sight!"[1]

The lyrics above are from a 1988 Top 40 platinum-selling song by Rob Base and DJ E-Z Rock, who initially made the song with samples from another song written in 1972 by James Brown and performed by Lyn Collins called "Think (About It)." You don't remember that? OK, then check out the lyrics to the 1965 hit song "It Takes Two," sung by Marvin Gaye and Kim Weston.

These lyrics succinctly sum up my convictions as a leader. Over the last 20 years, I have served in various executive leadership positions, from the federal government to the nonprofit sector to the corporate world and in ministry; and I felt the need to share experiences—mine and those of others—who have contributed to the success of those organizations in my companion book, *It Takes 2: Who Is Helping You Lead?*

I am a firm believer that it does take two (and three, and four, and more) to make things go right in an organization. Whether in the corporate world, nonprofit organizations, government, sports, entertainment, and the church, no one man or woman can build a winning tradition without help.

Tell me about a Steve Jobs, and I can show you a Steve Wozniak. If the greatest basketball player of all times is Michael Jordan, then I would say he never won a ring until Scottie Pippen matured as his sidekick. Show me a Bishop T. D. Jakes, and I can introduce you to a Pastor Lawrence Robinson. Explain to me the magnitude of the Civil Rights Movement lead by Dr. Martin Luther King Jr., and I can talk to you about Dr. Ralph Abernathy and Bayard Rustin. You might have heard of Warren Buffet, but I can tell you about Charles Munger, who serves as his 2Man and is a billionaire as well.

Let's go even further as we think about great leaders in the Bible. Moses had Aaron, Hur, and Joshua. Elijah had Elisha. David had Jonathan and Joab. Jesus had the disciples. You have a CEO, supervisor, or leader; but who is helping him lead? Get the picture? It may take one to lead a great organization, but it takes two to make it out of sight.

My objective in writing *It Takes 2* was a dual one: to help senior leaders (whom I refer to as 1s) understand the importance of having quality executive support leaders on their team and to identify how to find them. I want to inspire and encourage those who serve in executive leadership support roles (whom I affectionately refer to as 2men, or 2s) to embrace their uniqueness in helping lead their organizations from the second, third, or fourth chair.

How to Use This Workbook

This workbook was designed to help you to do inductive due diligence and research so that you can have all the necessary tools to be successful in your role. Each chapter will require you to respond to questions or to collect information from others to help you.

At the end of each chapter is an answer key to fill in the blanks; and there is a segment called "Take 2," which is designed to help you to reflect on what you've read before moving to the next chapter. I've included a page for journal notes, where you can write your thoughts and action items.

I believe that the critical discipline of a leader is the practice of reflection through journaling. Journaling allows you to record your thoughts and to develop strategic action plans for the implementation of what you learn from this book.

---

[1] "It Takes 2," written by Robert Ginyard, performed by Rob Base and DJ E-Z Rock, from the album *It Takes Two* (Profile Records, August 1988).

CHAPTER TWO

DO YOU KNOW?

1 Corinthians 12:4-7, 12-27

1 Corinthians 12 shows us that the church (or organization) is to function as a unified body. Everyone has a role to play, and each part is important. The eye isn't trying to be the hand. The ear doesn't envy the foot. The heart doesn't want to be an ear. It's clear that each part understands the value of the other members and wants and needs each part to function properly. Likewise, it is important that we are not ambiguous when it comes to our organization.

Know Your Leader
Leadership Assessment

The first step to being an effective 2man is _____ and _____ the leader of your organization, who we refer to as the _____. Is your #1 an _____ like Michael Jordan; or is he an _____ like Lebron James, looking to get everyone involved, or a _____, like Jason Kidd? Is your #1 a Moses, _____ in style; or is he a Joshua, _____? Is she more like the apostle Paul, _____ and _____; or is she _____ like Simon (later known as Peter)? Is he _____ like King Saul or _____ like King David?

Knowing the answers to these questions is important for you to determine what type of leader you're following, because as a 2, your _____ is to complement the 1s by providing help in the areas where they may be _____, or covering areas they don't want or don't know need to be covered. If you aren't sure who your leader is and what role he or she will play, or if your leader isn't sure, then you might not be the 2.

The Bible says, "And we beseech you, brethren, to know them which labor among you, and are over you in the Lord, and admonish you" (1 Thessalonians 5:12, KJV). Don't _____ the need for this critical set of instructions, because just as important as it is for you as a 2man to know who you are (which we will deal with later), in order to be a great help to your leader, you need to know who he or she is. My pastor, Dharius Daniels is a Joshua-type personality, an apostolic leader, a visionary, a teacher, a coach, a strategist, and a delegator. In order for me to help him execute the vision, I need to know as much about him as possible so that I can _____ him.

Chapter Two

For this section, I encourage you to interview the senior leader (or direct supervisor) in your organization and ask the following questions. This will be beneficial in helping you get his or her perspectives on how you can help your leader.

What are your top three spiritual gifts?

What are your bottom three spiritual gifts?

What is your personality type (DISC or Myer Briggs, for example)?

What are the greatest challenges that you face in leading our organization?

In your own words, how would you define my role?

If someone else occupied this role before me, why did he or she leave (if applicable)?

What is your style of leadership? (For example, micro-manager, delegator).

What are the major goals and objectives that you want me to focus on this year?

What does a successful working relationship between us look like?

How important is personal development for you and your staff?

Answer Key for Fill-in-the-Blank Assessment
knowing, understanding, #1, aggressive lion, all-around player, distributor, diplomatic, warrior-like, straightforward, driven, wishy-washy, insecure, purpose-driven, ultimate goal, weak, underestimate, complement

Know the Vision
Vision Interpretation

The second thing we must know is the _____ of our organization. 1 Corinthians 12 talks about the parts are joined together for a_____ by the same Spirit. This is God's vision for working as a _____. So, the questions we must ask ourselves are, *What is our common purpose? What is our vision?* In a video blog I started a few years ago entitled *Your Vision in 60 Seconds,* I compare vision to the picture on the front of a _____. It's a picture of _____; but in order to make the vision a reality, the _____ on the box must be followed. If you want the cake pictured on the box, you must follow the instructions printed on the back. This applies to your organization as well. As a staff or a team member in your organization, it is _____ that you take time not only to know the mission and vision statements verbatim, but also to _____ what those statements mean. You should be able to recite the statements, goals, and priorities of your organization in your own words to help others understand them.

Complete this section using your organization's important documents.

Write your organization's vision and mission statements below.

Chapter Two

If you only had 15 seconds to describe your organization's vision, what would you say to someone who knew nothing about it?

Write your organization's short-term and long-term goals below.

Write your organization's philosophy and/or strategies for achieving success?

On your organization's hierarchical organizational chart, who reports to whom?

At your leadership level, how are decisions made in your organization? Are there procedures in place for proposals and purchases?

Answer Key for Fill-in-the-Blank Assessment
vision, common purpose, team, cake box, possibility, instructions, imperative, process

Know Thyself
Self-Assessment

Revisit the foundational Scripture to help you understand the third thing you must know.

Even so the body is not made up of one part but of many. Now if the foot should say, "Because I am not a hand, I do not belong to the body," it would not for that reason stop being part of the body. And if the ear should say, "Because I am not an eye, I do not belong to the body," it would not for that reason stop being part of the body. If the whole body were an eye, where would the sense of hearing be? If the whole body were an ear, where would the sense of smell be? But in fact God has placed the parts in the body, every one of them, just as he wanted them to be. If they were all one part, where would the body be? (1 Corinthians 12:14-19)

As you read this, you get the overall concept of the need to work _____ as a team, all parts are important. But for this next exercise, it's important to dig a little deeper. When I read this passage, I see that the foot knows that it's not a hand. The ear isn't _____ and doesn't think that it is an eye. Likewise, the eye _____ that it is not the ear. And so on and so on. What's the point? The point is that each part of the body knows itself. Staying with the vision/cake box analogy mentioned above, remember that you can't bake a cake without the _____ ingredients. You need ingredients, such as eggs, oil, milk, and frosting, among others. So take a moment and ask yourself, *What am I?* Are you the egg, the oil, the milk, or the frosting? In the book, I talk about the types of 2men and women.

In your role as a 2, 3, 4, or whatever your role may be, you need to know who you are. William Shakespeare said, "_____." You will need to find out who you are and what God called and _____ you to do before you can successfully work in your role as a support leader. By understanding your _____ gift mixes and personality traits, you can better understand how God made you.

Before we move to the next chapter, I recommend that you stop here and take time to complete a spiritual gifts assessment and a personality test. And if you are called to ministry, then complete the five-fold gifting survey to help give you better insight.

Spiritual Gifts Assessment: spiritualgiftstest.com
Personality Test: 123test.com/disc-personality-test/
Five-Fold Ministry: fivefoldsurvey.com

Chapter Two

Take 2

What are your top three spiritual gifts?

What are your bottom three spiritual gifts?

What is your personality type (DISC, Myer Briggs, for example)?

What is your top five-fold ministry gift?

Why is understanding the vision and mission of your organization important to your success?

What did you learn about your leader that you didn't know before?

Why do you think it is so important to know your leader's gifts, personality, and leadership style?

Answer Key for Fill-in-the-Blank Assessment
together, confused, understands, necessary, "To thine own self be true," purposed, unique

JOURNAL REFLECTIONS

CHAPTER THREE

TYPES OF 2S

As I was preparing to write this book, I searched the Bible and identified key 2s and executive support staff persons, making note of the qualities that made them special, their spiritual gifts, personality traits, and the type of 2men they were. The profile of key 2s developed from my research is available for free at www.2mansupport.com, but I encourage you to take time to study these persons and discover which characters you most closely relate to. Understanding these biblical characters has brought me clarity in how God wants me to help my #1.

Seven Types of 2s
Armor-Bearer

The **Armor-Bearer** is one who brings relief and lightens the load for his or her #1. When most people hear the term *armor-bearer*, they think of a personal assistant in the corporate world who serves as an administrative assistant and who doubles as a nanny or a house sitter as well. Because the focus of this book is on 2man executives, I am not referring to those roles, even though a 2man may do all of that at times.

Here are a few questions to ask yourself to determine if you are an Armor-Bearer for your leader:

Do you look at the projects the #1 has and ask to handle some of those things so he or she can focus on the things that only leaders can do? **Yes or No**

Do you ask, "Can I handle a few of those meetings for you because your schedule is full?" **Yes or No**

Does your leader have multiple phone calls to return? Do you volunteer to make them? **Yes or No**

If the answer to all of these questions is yes, more than likely you are an Armor-Bearer.

Consultant

The **Consultant** is one who advises a leader on decisions. Discussion of this role is the essence of Richard Hytner's book *Consiglieri: Leading From the Shadows*. When most people think of the term *consigliere* (singular), they think of the term made popular in the movie trilogy *The Godfather*. In the mafia, the consigliere, or "counselor," is the man who advises the mob boss, sits in on meetings, and negotiates deals on the boss's behalf. The consigliere is not considered a threat to the boss's position because he serves his boss's best interests through his role as chancellor or counselor.

Here are a few questions to ask yourself to determine if you are a Consultant to your leader:

Does your leader come to you for advice before making major decisions? **Yes or No**

In your company, are you often the only person who is able to challenge a leader's decisions? **Yes or No**

Do you often play devil's advocate to make sure the best decisions are made for the organization? **Yes or No**

Do you often find yourself doing research or due diligence on new projects in order to brief your leader before he or she makes the final decision? **Yes or No**

If the answer to all four questions is yes, more than likely you are a Consultant.

Friend

The **Friend** is the 2man who serves as a trusted confidant and friend to the leader. One of the clearest illustrations of a Friend can be found in the relationship between the biblical characters Jonathan and David. Jonathan was the son of King Saul and heir apparent to the throne by birth. Although he was next in line to become a #1, he befriended a young man named David, who at the time served as an armor-bearer to the king.

Here are a few questions to ask yourself to determine if you are a Friend to your leader:

Do you often look out for your #1, despite the odds? **Yes or No**

Are you willing to spare your own job security in order to secure his or her well-being? **Yes or No**

Does your leader confide in you about sensitive matters and trust that his or her secrets will remain confidential? **Yes or No**

Do you make your leader's success your top priority, even at the risk of not being as successful yourself? **Yes or No**

If the answer to all four questions is yes, more than likely you are a Friend in the organization.

Executioner

An **Executioner's** job is to execute strategies developed by the #1, and he or she typically takes responsibility for delivering results on a day-to-day basis. As an Executioner, you live out this role in two ways: You execute the vision of your leader, and you execute all resistance to that vision. On many occasions, you are the one responsible for delivering the bad news or firing employees. (I'm sorry. *Repositioning of purpose transactions* is the more politically-correct term.) The role of Executioner is not an easy one to play because you become the "leader they love to hate," and it doesn't come with much fanfare.

Here are a few questions to ask yourself to determine if you are an Executioner for your leader:

Do you often play the bad cop role to your leader's good cop role in the organization? **Yes or No**

Do you often find yourself the one assigned to deliver bad news to other employees? **Yes or No**

Do you enforce policies and procedures as part of your job? **Yes or No**

Do you take the decided-upon action plans from meetings and execute them to perfection? **Yes or No**

If the answer to all four questions is yes, more than likely you are an Executioner.

Interpreter

An **Interpreter** is one who explains or presents something in understandable terms. He or she brings to realization by demonstration. Interpreters translate the visionary's plan and makes it plain. Visionaries need help interpreting their visions and communicating them effectively with employees, congregations, vendors, and community partners. So Interpreters are strategists and organizational architects who work alongside their leaders to help develop systems and plans that bring visions to pass.

Here are a few questions to ask yourself to determine if you are an Interpreter to your leader:

Does your leader come to you when thinking about developing new ideas or plans? **Yes or No**

Does your leader lean on you to help him or her make ideas practical for others? **Yes or No**

Are you invited to brainstorming meetings when new initiatives are in development stages? **Yes or No**

Are you able to take your leader's ideas and then conduct research on the subject matter and come back with plans on how to execute from concept to completion? **Yes or No**

If the answer to all four questions is yes, then you are more than likely an Interpreter.

Partner

In some sense, all 2s partner with their 1s to help bring the vision of the organization to pass, but there are some people who may serve more as a **Partner** than any other role. They share the same level of responsibility for the success of the organization, may have started the organization with the 1s, and/or are an irreplaceable component of the organization. There aren't many people who serve in this capacity alone, but they do exist.

Here are a few questions to ask yourself to determine if you are a Partner to your leader:

Are you an essential component and a creator of the vision and the mission of the organization? **Yes or No**

Is it unlikely that the assignment can be completed without you? **Yes or No**

Do you have an influential voice in the organization? **Yes or No**

Do you have the same pressure as your leader to ensure the organization is successful? **Yes or No**

Do you have equal stake and investment in the organization as the leader? **Yes or No**

If you answered yes to all five questions, more than likely you are a Partner.

Successor

Successors are those who serve as 2s for a period of time but who will eventually succeed their 1s and become a 1 in their own right. Some Successors come into this position with the goal of eventually becoming a 1, and they use this position as a stepping stone to that role. Others may become a Successor without even seeking the position but have served faithfully in their 2man role. They possess all the necessary qualities of a 2, such as humility, loyalty, and excellence; and when their leaders are ready to transition, they can't think of anyone else who would be more qualified to replace them, so the Successor becomes the leader.

Here are a few questions to ask yourself to determine if you are a Successor to your leader:

Has it been clearly communicated that you are next in line for the position? **Yes or No**

Are you being trained and developed to take on more high-level responsibilities? **Yes or No**

Are the people in your department aware that you will one day lead them? **Yes or No**

If the answer to all three questions is yes, more than likely you are a Successor.

After reading about what a 2man is and the various roles he or she may play, let me leave you with the greatest example. When I think of what it means to be a 2man, I find the greatest example is not Joseph, Barnabas, or any other person. The best example is Jesus.

God is #1 and needed an Executioner to carry out His plans. Philippians 2:6-8 (NIV) says, "Who, being in very nature God, did not consider equality with God something to be used to his own advantage; rather, he made himself nothing by taking the very nature of a servant, being made in human likeness. And being found in appearance as a man, he humbled himself by becoming obedient to death—even death on a cross!" Jesus came down from His Partner role and became an Executioner.

The hope for the faithful 2man is that, eventually, God will take notice of your service. Despite the fact that you might not receive accolades from your peers and from those you serve, God sees and will elevate you in due time.

Take 2

List the type of 2 you normally play in the organization (maximum of 3 types)

What did you learn about the role(s) that you play in your organization?

What do you see as the greatest benefit to your leader when you successfully play your role?

JOURNAL REFLECTIONS

CHAPTER FOUR

THE QUALITIES OF A 2

In writing *It Takes 2: Who Is Helping You Lead?* I thought about my journey and experiences and asked myself, *What are some of the key qualities of a 2man?* The answer came in the form of an acronym: H.O.R.S.E.

For this illustration, the horse is used as a metaphor and an acronym. In Chapter 3 of my book, I list key facts about horses that will help you understand this comparison better. So how can you take on more of a horse's best qualities and serve your lion more effectively? Consider the following attributes that make up a H.O.R.S.E.

For each quality listed below, rate yourself on a scale of 1 to 10. Honestly assess your current status as it relates to this quality. Note: Don't just rate yourself based on what you think. Instead, rate yourself based on answers you receive from your leader and your peers. How would they rate you? Circle the correct answer.

Humility: The top quality of a great executive leader is humility. Humility requires you to put others' needs before your own without expecting to receive credit or applause for your accomplishments.
1-2-3-4-5-6-7-8-9-10

Health. Only healthy, emotionally secure people can be humble. Health, in this context, refers to all categories of health, such as physical, emotional, relational, financial, and mental.
1-2-3-4-5-6-7-8-9-10

Obedient. Executive leaders complete the tasks assigned quickly and efficiently. However, their obedience is not just about checking items off their never-ending to-do lists. As a horse, the executive leader is obedient and willing to be led.
1-2-3-4-5-6-7-8-9-10

Organized. All of your organizational tools can be on your phone or tablet. It's important for an executive leader to write and execute goals with precision. You use a calendar strategically to ensure you accomplish tasks and manage projects on a yearly, quarterly, monthly, weekly, and daily basis. The projects and assignments you work on will vary, so you must be able to organize yourself in a way that will help you be most effective.
1-2-3-4-5-6-7-8-9-10

Resourceful. When your leader can come to you with a new project that requires you to leverage relationships and networks to get the job done faster than anyone else, then you continue to make yourself valuable to your organization.
1-2-3-4-5-6-7-8-9-10

Resilience. You recover quickly from difficulties because you have a tough skin. You will make mistakes. You will be disappointed and hurt, but resilience is the ability to bounce back.
1-2-3-4-5-6-7-8-9-10

Submitted. In Chapter 5 of his book *RePresent Jesus*, Dr. Dharius Daniels describes the importance of the "S-word." Often, people try to avoid the word *submission* because they associate it with weakness. But submission isn't weakness; it simply means to get under the mission for the sake of the team!
1-2-3-4-5-6-7-8-9-10

Strategic. An executive leader is strategic in thinking and time management. You employ a strategic skill set to assist your leader to interpret their visions and transform them into reality.
1-2-3-4-5-6-7-8-9-10

Excellent. While serving as a consultant for Dr. Timothy W. Sloan, pastor of The Luke Church in Humble, Texas, I heard the slogan "Efficiency + Effectiveness = Excellence." The combination of efficiency and effectiveness equates to excellence. But excellence is more than what you do; it is the way you think. In fact, excellence is 90 percent mental and only ten percent mechanical.
1-2-3-4-5-6-7-8-9-10

Example. Your example is one of the greatest assets you can bring to the organization. Your leader needs someone to point to who embodies the culture traits, core values, and excellence in which he or she want others to operate. As an example, your actions, in most cases, will speak louder than your words.
1-2-3-4-5-6-7-8-9-10

Confidentiality
As a 2man, you will more than likely serve as chief of staff, or leader of leaders, which means you will be privy to sensitive information. Your leader will share things with you in confidence that you can never repeat to anyone. Many times, you will see your leader at his or her most vulnerable and human state, and you will need to keep him or her covered. You may be exposed to your leader's flaws and weaknesses and need to help him or her manage. Are you able to see and hear confidential information and still serve?
1-2-3-4-5-6-7-8-9-10

Loyalty
"Loyalty is tested by how you respond to offense and how you respond to opportunities." Brian Houston, senior pastor of Hillsong Church in Sydney, New South Wales, Australia, shared this statement with my pastor, Dr. Dharius Daniels, and other leaders while they were in New Zealand. Loyalty is a serious

issue, and you have to be clear on what God is calling you to do and to whom He is calling you to serve because sometimes the lines get blurry.

1-2-3-4-5-6-7-8-9-10

Take 2

Of the qualities listed above, what are your three strongest?

What qualities do you need to work on the most?

What did you learn about yourself while studying the H.O.R.S.E.-like qualities?

List a time when you had to be confidential in your role? What was the potential danger in not keeping the information confidential?

List a time when your loyalty was tested in your organization? Did it involve you being offended or another opportunity being presented to you? Explain.

Do the people in your organization view you as a loyal person?

JOURNAL REFLECTIONS

CHAPTER FIVE

THE MOTIVATIONS OF A 2

Motivation is the reason for a person's _____ or _____, and sometimes it can be a _____. Motivation often drives _____, good and bad. So although a person is motivated, that doesn't mean his or her actions will result in _____.

Wrong Motivations

Serving in an executive leadership support role in any organization requires you to be _____ in every aspect of your life. You will experience many _____ situations, such as peer pressure, lack of recognition, lack of appreciation, lack of exposure, disrespect from team members and family, feelings of not being enough, anxiety, and stress—just to name a few. So good health and _____ must be in your toolkit. The 2man role is not a role you take on in order to address your unmet needs of affirmation, security, or esteem.

What are some of the wrong motivations that a person can have in an organization?

Right Motivations

My list of right motivations for serving as a 2man is short and simple: (A) You're called to it, (B) you have a love for the leader who needs your support, (C) you have a love and a passion for seeing the vision of that organization come to pass, or (D) a combination of any of the above. I would go so far as to say that it should be A, B, and C; but sometimes you can start with one and grow into the others. Read the descriptions of each of these areas in Chapter 5 of the book, and then return to complete this next assessment.

Called

Prior to working where you are now, did you sense an inner inspiration to provide the type of services or products that your current organization provides? **Yes or No**

Since working with your current organization, have you felt a sense of fulfillment that is unlike any other job you have held before? **Yes or No**

When you finish your assignment for the day, no matter how long or difficult, do you feel accomplished? Do you look forward to going back the next day? **Yes or No**

Do you feel as if your organization taps into and makes the best use of your unique skills and gifts? **Yes or No**

Do you ever feel as if you know how to handle certain things in your organization instinctively without ever having learned it before? **Yes or No**

If you answered yes to at least three of these questions, you are called to be part of this organization.

Love for the Leader
Do you want to see your leader win in ways a normal person does not? **Yes or No**

When you hear your leader speak, hear who he or she is, and what he or she is trying to accomplish, do you feel as if you were born to help your leader? **Yes or No**

Did you know upon meeting or listening to the leader of the organization speak that you were meant to help him or her? **Yes or No**

If the leader of your organization announced that he or she was leaving to start something new, would you feel led to go with your leader? **Yes or No**

Have you had to defend your #1's decision and behavior to other people inside or outside of the organization? **Yes or No**

If you answered yes to at least three of these questions, you have a unique love and a dedication to your leader.

Passion for the Vision
Steve Jobs said, "If you are working on something that you really care about, you don't have to be pushed. The vision pulls you."

Do you find yourself not being able to sleep at night because you are thinking about ideas and strategies to achieve your organization's goals? **Yes or No**

When you hear new plans and goals in your organization, do you begin researching what other organizations are doing that are similar because you want to find the best ways to achieve them? **Yes or No**

Are you constantly presenting new ideas to your organization on ways to improve processes? **Yes or No**

Do you find yourself clarifying your organization's vision to others who don't understand it? **Yes or No**

Are you obsessed with the desire to see your organization's vision and mission become a reality? **Yes or No**

If you answered yes to at least three of these questions, you have a unique passion to see your organization's vision become a reality.
Note: Be careful of jumping out of place and desiring a position that you may not be called or equipped to handle. If you're producing fruit in your role as a 2man, your team is winning, and you're being recognized for your contributions, then maybe you should consider blooming where you're planted.

Take 2
What is motivating you in your current position? (Circle One)
I am called to do this
My love for my leader
My passion for the vision
All of the above

Was there a time when you knew how to handle certain things instinctively without ever learning about it? Explain.

Can you remember the moment when you knew that you were dedicated to your leader? What happened?

Think of a time recently when you stayed up late or went above and beyond your job duties to ensure your organization accomplished a goal or an objective. Explain.

Answer Key for Fill-in-the-Blank Assessment
actions, desires, two-edged sword, behavior, good consequences, healthy, negative, pure motives

JOURNAL REFLECTIONS

CHAPTER SIX

CRITICAL SUCCESS TOOLS

You've been selected for this role. You understand who you are and what the role requires, and you have the qualities necessary to be a solid 2man. The next step is to receive proper training.

Critical Success Tools
In addition to the training needed for a 2man, there are other critical tools you need in order to do your job at a high level. Those tools, which are critical to your success are clarity, support, honesty, direct communication, leadership, and resources.

Clarity. This is the most important and valuable gift your leader can give you.

On a scale of 1 to 10, how clear are you on the vision of your organization?
On a scale of 1 to 10, how clear are you on the expectations for your position?
On a scale of 1 to 10, how clear are you on the goals and objectives for this year?
On a scale of 1 to 10, how clear are you on the dos and don'ts that will help you survive and thrive in this role?
Total (max 40):
If your total number is lower than 30, then I recommend that you meet with your supervisor immediately and get more clarity to help you fulfill your role effectively.

Support. Serving in a 2man role isn't easy. Sometimes you have to be the bad cop, the bearer of bad news, and the leader they love to hate. So it's important that you have support from the top when you are going out to the wolves.

On a scale of 1 to 10, rate the level of support you receive from your leader.
If your number is lower than 6, write out the specific support you need. All of us have different love languages, such as affirmation and gifts, for example. What type of support do you need?

Once you are clear on the type of support you need, assess how realistic it is to expect that from your leader. Is he or she able to provide that support? Determine if there is some other way or someone else from whom you can receive the type of support you need (consider joining a network such as www.2mansupport.com). Then, discuss the kind of support you need from your leader in order to be more productive.

Honesty. As a 2man, if you're going down the wrong path, not doing well, or your leader wants something more out of you, then he or she needs to be honest and let you know.

On a scale of 1 to 10, how much honest feedback does your leader provide you?
If your number is lower than 6, I recommend that you go to your leader and ask him or her to give you honest feedback that will help you to be more productive.
Note: Remember, one quality of a 2man is health. You have to be emotionally healthy in order to receive frequent honest assessments of yourself.

Direct Communication. In order to execute your #1's directives, you need direct communication and not second-hand information, where the message can be filtered or altered. If you are responsible for carrying out the execution of a plan, then that information should come straight from the top and not from one of your leader's subordinates.

On a scale of 1 to 10, how well does your leader provide direct communication to you about information that impacts you or your performance directly?
If your total number is lower than 6, then you may have a real problem. Most leaders only begin to work around you when they have lost trust in your productivity. I recommend doing an honest self-assessment to determine what is going on. If your #1 went from speaking to you frequently to not speaking to you, find out why.

Leadership. You are called to serve your #1, but you are not just a worker to carry out the mission. Instead, you should be an object of the mission.

On a scale of 1 to 10, do you feel as if you are being properly led in your organization?

Resources. In order to be effective, you need to be equipped with personal and organizational resources so that you can carry out your job.

On a scale of 1 to 10, do you feel as if you have the appropriate resources to do your job?

On a scale of 1 to 10, do you feel as if you are adequately compensated for the work that you do?

On a scale of 1 to 10, do you feel as if you have opportunities for development via conferences, training, or coaching, for example?

Total (max 30):

If your total number is lower than 20, I recommend that you begin to research ways to obtain the proper resources in order to help fulfill your role better.

Flexibility. A great 2man is always on call and ready to move at any time when needed (H.O.R.S.E.), therefore flexibility in your schedule may be important.

On a scale of 1 to 10, how much flexibility do you have in your schedule?

Public Affirmation of Delegated Authority. I have seen many mistakes made by 1s in not providing this affirmation. If the 2man is going to have authority, then the team and those involved need to hear the leader publicly declare it.

On a scale of 1 to 10, how well does your leader provide public affirmation of your authority in the organization to the rest of the team?

Take 2
In the space below, reflect on and explain your orientation process when you came into your role.

Out of the three areas of knowledge required to be successful, which one do you think is most important? Why?

Which critical success tools did you get the most of when starting in your position?

Which critical success tools do you need from your leader to help you now?

JOURNAL REFLECTIONS

CHAPTER SEVEN

WHAT ABOUT ME?

The Challenges of Being a 2

I have seen how failure in managing this area has destroyed great 2s, and my prayer is that it never happens to any one of us. Many challenges come with this role, including isolation, jealousy, envy from team members, successful management of our ambition, limited spousal support or pressure from them for us to pursue other career paths, a lack of outlets for us to vent, and a neglect of self-care. The struggles with right motives and unmet needs can destroy us as well.

What About My Dreams?

The next challenge is answering the question you might ask yourself, *What do I do with my own vision, dreams, and aspirations?* On multiple occasions along this journey, I have had to wrestle with my own desires, ambitions, and dreams that I knew were from God.

" 'Truly I tell you,' Jesus said to them, 'no one who has left home or wife or brothers or sisters or parents or children for the sake of the kingdom of God will fail to receive many times as much in this age, and in the age to come eternal life' " (Luke 18:29-30).

Earlier, we stated that one of the keys to being a great 2man is knowing yourself. You already completed the gifts and personality assessments, so here are a few more questions to help you discover your own dreams.

Given your gifts and personality traits, what makes you uniquely different?

What are your strengths?

What bothers or upsets you?

Chapter Seven

What drives you?

If you could do one thing to change the world, what would it be?

What do you want to be remembered for?

How Is Your Mental Health?
Speaking of self-care, 2men must also overcome challenges with their mental and emotional health. What can we as 2s do to take better care of ourselves and stand up under the pressures we face? Consider the following suggestions:[1]

Seek counseling. This is going to require work, venturing outside of your comfort zone and interviewing counselors until you get the right fit.

On a scale of 1 to 10, how likely are you to seek counseling?

Set aside time for yourself. Identify a sabbath, a 24-hour period where you are not engaging in anything work-related.

On a scale of 1 to 10, rate the quality of time you set aside for yourself?

Develop good sleep habits. Research shows that anything less than four hours a night for extended periods of time can lead to irritability, lack of focus and productivity, anxiousness, increased fatigue, and increased stress, which can induce other health complications.

On a scale of 1 to 10, how good is your sleep?

Attend to medical concerns immediately and effectively.

On a scale of 1 to 10, rate your overall medical health.

Develop a regular eating schedule (make better food choices) and a workout regimen.

On a scale of 1 to 10, rate your overall health (diet and exercise)?

If you are married and/or have children, restructure your schedule so you can invest time with those you love and those who love you.

On a scale of 1 to 10, rate the quality of time you spend with your spouse and children on a weekly basis.

I hope this gives you greater insight into at least some of the things that you, or those you serve with, can do to get in front of challenges before they start. This must be done for us to be effective and efficient in the roles we serve. I pray that we take our families, our self-care, and our issues seriously and do the work necessary to allow us to flourish and to be fruitful as 2men and women. If you want help, then our network is a resource for you, as we walk through these deep waters together.

[1]Contributed by Verily Harper, LPC.

Take 2
In the book *The Power and Purpose of Vision*, Dr. Myles Munroe tells a story about an interview that the great humanitarian Hellen Keller told Walter Cronkite. He asked her what could be worse than being blind. She replied that the only thing worse than being blind is being born with eyes but having no vision. Vision is the most important and valuable asset we have.

Describe the vision for your life?

What are you doing to fulfill it?

When will you engage in sabbath?

Who are the people you can talk to for coaching? for counseling? for mentoring?

JOURNAL REFLECTIONS

CHAPTER EIGHT

THE 2MAN AND HIS FAMILY

Serving as a 2man doesn't just impact _____ and your _____; it also affects your _____. Your story may not be like anyone else's, but you will still need to prepare for the _____ that will come through your family when you accept the call to be a 2man. Here are some tips to help you _____ your family and be a good 2.

First, make sure you and your spouse are on the same page as it relates to the calling and assignment on your life, preferably before you get married, if at all possible. If it's too late for that, then it's time to sit down and have a real conversation about who you are and where you see yourself going in the future.

Have a conversation with your spouse about what you feel called to do with your life and career. Journal here about the conversation. Were any discoveries made? Did he or she already know? Is he or she OK with it? Do they have knowledge, skills, or resources that can help you in this area?

Second, give more effort and attention to your spouse and family than ever before. Serving as a 2man means you become a suitable helpmeet to your leader, in the way we expect a spouse to be. Therefore, your family shouldn't be made to feel that you appreciate, sacrifice, love, and serve your #1 and his or her family more than you do your own.

Take time to discuss with your spouse and children how they feel you are doing with prioritizing them and balancing your work and family life. Journal here about the conversation.

Third, set balance and boundaries by developing an annual, quarterly, monthly, weekly, and daily plan; then communicate that with your family.

Annual Planning. With your spouse, plan your vacations and other activities for the year. Write out your important annual dates here:

Wedding anniversary:

List the birthday of your immediate family and close friends:

List your spring break weeks (if applicable):

List possible vacation times:

List other important dates:

Chapter Eight

Quarterly Planning

List spouse's important dates:

List children's important dates:

List important work-related project due dates and/or events:

Monthly Planning

List doctor's appointments:

List children's sports and recreational activities:

List work-related project priorities for the month:

Weekly Planning

List meetings for the week and resources needed:

List messages to be returned:

List priorities for the week:

Plan a date night with your spouse for the week:

Take time to develop your weekly plan (what days will you handle certain priorities):

Answer Key for Fill-in-the-Blank Assessment

you, organization, family, warfare, balance

JOURNAL REFLECTIONS

CHAPTER NINE

FINAL REFLECTIONS

"It takes 2 to make a thing go right! It takes 2 to make it out of sight!"

List three things you have learned as a result of reading the book *It Takes 2* and completing this workbook.

What are two immediate take-aways from this book?

List action steps you plan to take as a result of this information?

Overall, how can you become a better 2man to your current leader?

Think of your prior support roles. How could that experience have been different if you had known then what you know now after reading this book?

2Man Scoring Guide
Transfer all of your scores from the previous chapters here, and then total them to determine your ultimate 2Man Leadership Score.

Qualities of a 2 Scores
    Humility _____
    Health _____
    Obedient _____
    Organized _____
    Resourceful
    Resilient _____
    Submitted _____
    Strategic _____
    Excellent _____
    Example _____
    Confidentiality _____
    Loyalty _____
    Total (max 120) _____

Critical Success Tools
    Clarity (total) _____
    Support _____
    Honesty _____
    Direct Communication _____
    Leadership _____
    Resources (total) _____
    Flexibility _____
    Public Affirmation _____
    Total (max 130) _____

Chapter Nine

How Is Your Mental Health?
- Counseling _____
- Rest _____
- Sleep _____
- Medical Health _____
- General Health (Diet/Exercise) _____
- Quality Family Time _____
- Total (max 60) _____

2Man Total (max 310):

What Type of 2Man/H.O.R.S.E. Are You?
Scale

A: Mare(F) or Stallion (M) 279 or higher
Congratulations, you are a mature, experienced, well-rounded, and established 2Man. You are in a position to reproduce or coach others. Mares and Stallions are adult horses that are ready for breeding. You are also ready and have the capacity to help someone else's vision and develop your own. The downside to these horses are they are known to be cranky or unwilling to yield, so be careful of getting stuck in your ways. Remember, humility must be one of the key qualities of a 2Man.

B: Filly (F) or Colt (M) 248–278
Congratulations, you are doing well as a 2Man and blossoming in your role. Although not fully comfortable and settled in the role, you are on your way to a long and rewarding career as a 2Man. As you continue to receive the right training and critical success tools, you will soon be at the next level and ready to coach others. It is important at this stage to make sure you protect your environment so you don't allow anyone to stunt your growth, to lose focus, or to try to coach others too soon.

C: Yearling (M or F) 217–247
In this stage, you have a lot of potential. You may be new to this position, so you need a lot of development. The critical success tools, the challenges of a 2Man, and the 2Man and his family are areas that you should make priority in this season. The upside is great, but don't allow disappointment, lack of encouragement, or selfish ambition to derail your career. The 2Man Coaching Network would be a perfect place for you to develop.

D: Foal 186–216
Don't worry if you are new to this role. Everyone has to start somewhere. At this stage, it is critical that you not only receive a lot of clarity and direction from your #1, but that you also connect with other peers to help you nurture and develop into this role properly. Like your horse counterpart, you are too young to be ridden hard and expected to carry too much of a load because this is a heavy development stage for you. If you are not new to this position, then I recommend that you speak to your #1 immediately to request setting up a developmental plan or request to be moved to another position that better suits your skill sets. The bright side is that maybe you are better suited eventually for a #1 spot!

F: This Isn't for You! 185 or less
Unfortunately, unless you are brand-new to this role, I recommend that you look for a position that better suits your skill sets. There is no such thing as wrong people, but simply wrong place. Again, you just may not have horse tendencies in you, and maybe this is helping you identify some roaring tendencies in your future!

About the Author

Ramone Harper
Ramone is the founder of BNB Consulting and Associates, a management and consulting firm that contracts with ministries, organizations, not-for-profits, and start-ups in the areas of business organization and development, staff and leadership development, and branding. He also serves as executive pastor at Change Church in Ewing, New Jersey, where he oversees all ministry operations and campus pastors and assists the lead pastor to interpret and strategically execute goals and objectives.

In 2016, Ramone co-authored the book *It Was All a Dream,* of which 100 percent of the proceeds go toward the Turning Dreams Into Realities (www.tdi2r.org) scholarship and mentoring nonprofit organization, where he serves as a founder and a board member. Ramone earned his BS in public relations with a minor in business administration from Alabama State University, where he graduated summa cum laude in 1997. He is currently enrolled at Regents University, working on his master of divinity degree. He was selected as one of the Ebony Men of the Year by Alpha Kappa Alpha Sorority, Inc., included in the 2013-2015 *Who's Who in Black Houston* publication as one of the top entrepreneurs, and honored as one of Houston's Top 50 Entrepreneurs in 2015.

Contributors

Verily Harris-Harper, LPC, NCC
Verily has found a way to combine over 16 years of professional and clinical experience. And her diverse experiences are described as nothing short of amazing, because good or bad, her perspective is that they were necessary and valuable aspects of the journey. What Verily was able to discover was paramount because she realized that the "best life" is an inside job. The "best life" begins with the "best self," and it is out of this discovery that TBE Global LLC was formed. The recipe is quite simple: "Small change, BIG IMPACT."

Verily graduated magna cum laude with a bachelor's degree in business management from LeTourneau University in Longview, Texas, and graduated with highest honors with a master's degree in mental health counseling from Capella University. Verily is a Nationally Certified Counselor, licensed in Texas and New Jersey.

Dr. Heather Jackson
Heather Jackson is an educator, writer, and curriculum developer. She has spent over 20 years in urban education working as a school and district administrator. Dr. Jackson loves to read, write, and exercise. She is a self-acknowledged "gym-rat." Dr. Jackson's book, *The Ten Things Instructional Coaches Must Do,* was published in 2005.

Chapter Nine

What You Can Expect From 2ManSupport.Com

In preparation for launching this book and this organization, I did a lot of research to find out if anything like it already existed. I would like to acknowledge the incredible work that people such as Beverly Robinson and Marjorie Duncan have done in developing the CEASE organization (www.cease admin.com), which is designed to provide support to executive administrative assistants and on whose advisory board I have the pleasure of serving.

I want to thank authors Mike Bonem and Roger Patterson (*Leading From the Second Chariot*); Jacquetta Smith (*Loyalty: The Pathway to Promotion*); and one of the best 2s that I have ever met, Terry Nance (*God's Armor Bearer*), who I reference often in this book. I read books such as *Consiglieri*, by Richard Hytner, which captures the essence and the spirit of a 2man in the corporate world. Richard did a great job in helping show the similarities that exist between a senior leader and his 2, the differences in their leadership styles, the types of 2s, and advice for each of these important leaders.

I won't try to restate what they wrote; but with this resource and corresponding coaching network (www.2mansupport.com), I'm attempting to pick up where they left off. I wanted to provide insight into the minds of 2s from one who has served in that capacity for many years for various leaders; give insight on the value and perspective from senior leaders who are the recipients of 2s' support but who have had to lead for various seasons without a capable 2; and to provide support, resources, and mentoring (which, to me, is the greatest missing link) to the many called, chosen, and sometimes hesitant 2s who are out there.

If you are interested in being part of the next 2Man coaching network cohort, visit our website and complete an interest form. We look forward to partnering with you to help you accelerate your growth in this unique role.

BIBLIOGRAPHY

Consiglieri: Leading From the Shadows, by Richard Hytner (Profile Books, 2014).

God's Armor Bearer: Serving God's Leaders, revised edition, by Terry Nance (Spirit-Filled Books, 2003). Nance served 23 years with Agape Church in Little Rock, Arkansas, as the senior associate and executive director of Agape Missionary Alliance. He is now president of Focus on the Harvest Ministries.

"Horse," Wikipedia (wikipedia.org/wiki/Horse).

It Takes 2: Who Is Helping You Lead, by Ramone Harper (Heritage Publishing, 2018).

Loyalty: The Pathway to Promotion, Working Up Close and Personal in Ministry, by Jacquetta Brown Smith (VJS Productions, Inc., 2003). Smith served as executive director at New Light Christian Center in Houston, Texas, under the leadership of Dr. I. V. Hilliard.

RePresent Jesus: Rethink Your Version of Christianity and Become More Like Christ, by Dharius Daniels (Charisma House, 2014).

The Emotionally Healthy Leader: How Transforming Your Inner Life Will Deeply Transform Your Church, Team, and the World, by Peter Scazzero (Zondervan, 2015).

www.ingramcontent.com/pod-product-compliance
Lightning Source LLC
Chambersburg PA
CBHW051425070526
44584CB00023B/3588